W9-AOU-287

Justin Timberlake

Dan Whitcombe

Raintree

Chicago, Illinois

Customer Service 888-363-4266

Visit our website at www.raintreelibrary.com

For more information address the publisher:
Raintree, 100 N. LaSalle, Suite 1200, Chicago IL 60602

Printed and bound in China by South China Printing Company

09 08 07 06 05
10 9 8 7 6 5 4 3 2 1

Library of Congress Cataloging-in-Publication Data:

Whitcombe, Dan.
  Justin Timberlake / Dan Whitcombe.
     p. cm. -- (Star files)
  Includes bibliographical references and index.
  ISBN 1-4109-1087-3 (library binding-hardcover)
  1. Timberlake, Justin, 1981---Juvenile literature 2. Singers--United States--Biography--
  Juvenile literature. I. Title. II. Series.
  ML3930.T58W5 2005
  782.42164'092--dc22

                              2004011294

Acknowledgements
The publishers would like to thank the following for permission to reproduce photographs: Corbis pp. **16**, **26** (r); Getty Images pp. **6** (t), **15** (t), **25**, **30**, **32** (r); Retna Pictures pp. **7** (t), **8–9**, **11** (l), **14**, **15** (b), **20**, **21** (t), **23** (t), **23** (b), **31** (r), **37**, **40** (l), **42**, **43** (r); Rex Features pp. **4**, **6** (b), **7** (b), **8**, **9**, **10**, **11** (r), **12**, **13** (l), **13** (r), **17** (t), **17** (b), **18**, **19** (l), **19** (r), **21** (b), **22** (l), **22** (r), **24** (l), **24** (r), **26** (l), **27** (l), **27** (r), **28**, **29** (l), **29** (r), **31** (l), **32** (l), **33**, **34**, **35** (l), **35** (r), **36**, **38**, **39** (l), **39** (r), **40**, **41**, **43** (l). Cover photograph reproduced with permission of Retna Pictures.

Quote sources p. **4** The *Observer Magazine*: 6 October 2002; p. **11** *USA Today*, 20 July 1999; p. **12** *Justin Timberlake: The Unofficial Book*, Martin Roach; p. **20** MTV interview, September 2002; p. **23** interview with groovevolt.com; p. **25** MTV interview, September 2002; p. **28** *Vibe* magazine, February 2003; p. **33** The *Guardian*, January 2003; p. **41** The *Herald* 25 January 2003; p. **42** VH1 interview, 18 November 2002; The *Guardian*, 31 January 2003.

The publishers would like to thank Voirrey Carr and Simone Apel for their assistance in the preparation of this book.

Disclaimer: This book is not authorized or approved by Justin Timberlake.

Contents

Some words are shown in bold, **like this**. You can find out what they mean by looking in the glossary. You can also look out for them in the "Star Words" box at the bottom of each p

Justin Crazy

ALL ABOUT JUSTIN

Full name: Justin Randall Timberlake
Born: 6.30pm, January 31, 1981
Place of birth: St. Jude's Medical Center, Memphis, Tennessee
Family: Randy (father); Lynn (mother); Paul Harless (stepfather); Lisa (stepmother); Jonathan and Stephen (half-brothers)
Height: 6' 1" (1.86 meters) **Eyes:** Blue
Hair: Sandy blond **Star sign:** Aquarius
Hobbies: Computer games, golf, basketball
Favorite musicians: Stevie Wonder, Michael Jackson, Marvin Gaye
Sports hero: Michael Jordan
First hit: "I Want You Back" with 'NSYNC
Other Interests: The Justin Timberlake Foundation, a music charity in Memphis

Justin Timberlake is one of the hottest properties in the pop world. He is very successful. Getting to the top was not easy, though. Justin has had to work hard for his breaks. Justin's career started when he was spotted on a television talent show. He was just eleven years old.

Music star

Justin has been a children's television presenter. He has been the lead singer in a very popular boy band. He has also been half of one of the biggest celebrity couples in the pop world. Now he has the world at his feet. What about the future?

⭐ Star fact

Justin's curly hair became his **trademark** when he was younger. Not everyone liked it, though. Justin admits that one of his nicknames was "brillo pad!"

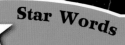

Justin could continue to become a great pop star. He could turn to music **production**. He may try becoming a movie star. With his talent and dedication, not even Justin knows what the future holds.

> **My boy is just what he is. He's got music.** (Pharrell Williams of the Neptunes)

Find out later

How old was Justin when 'NSYNC formed?

Who came up with the name of 'NSYNC and what does it stand for?

Which famous hip-hop **producer** has Justin worked with?

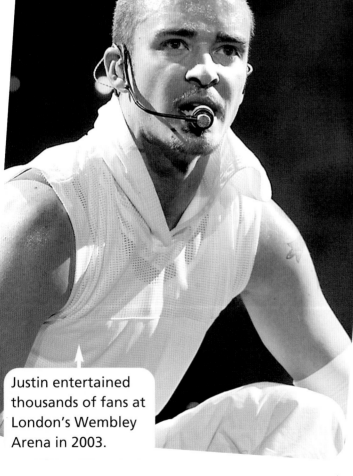

Justin entertained thousands of fans at London's Wembley Arena in 2003.

production arranging and mixing the music when recording a song

Starting Out

Justin was born in Memphis, Tennessee, in 1981. Music was part of his life from the beginning. Justin's mother, Lynn, played several instruments when she was young, and her father had been a bass player. Justin's father, Randy, was a famous **bluegrass** singer.

Home life

Justin's family lived in a respectable **suburb** of the town. His early life was not all easy, though. His parents separated when he was just two years old. Lynn remarried a banker named Paul Harless when Justin was four.

Justin and the rest of 'NSYNC show off their pets.

⭐ ⭐ ⭐ ⭐ ⭐ ⭐ ⭐ ⭐ ⭐

Justin's dogs

Two of the best reasons for Justin to spend time at his mother's house are the two family Yorkshire Terrier dogs. Their names are Bearlie and Bella, and they are both fans of Justin.

⭐ ⭐ ⭐ ⭐ ⭐ ⭐ ⭐ ⭐ ⭐

Memphis is famous for its blues musicians.

Star Words

bluegrass music that combines Irish and Scottish traditional music with that of the African-American slaves

Paul is the man that Justin thought of as his father when he was growing up. Randy also married again and had two more sons. These are Justin's half-brothers, Jonathan and Stephen.

Justin and his future manager-mom.

Memphis stars

Justin was not the first great musician to come out of Memphis. Other **icons** include the rock 'n' roll legend Jerry Lee Lewis. He had a huge hit with the song "Great Balls of Fire" in the 1950s. Memphis's most famous musician is "The King," Elvis Presley.

Elvis got his start in Memphis.

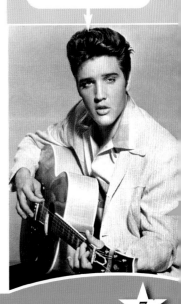

⭐ Star fact

MTV was launched in 1981. So Justin and one of the most famous television channels dedicated to music were born in the same year!

---

icon important or famous person that you look up to and try to be like

7

Singing always felt natural for Justin. As a child Justin sang at the services in the family's local Baptist church. At the age of eight he started singing lessons with a voice coach named Bob Westbrook. Justin and some of his friends even performed in a New Kids on the Block **tribute band** at school. Justin caused quite a stir with the girls at the concert. This was a taste of things to come!

Trying out

Justin wanted to be famous outside Memphis, however. From the age of nine he went on every talent show he could. One of his early performances was on the famous country music show The Grand Ole Opry.

First chance

When he was eleven, Justin got his biggest chance yet. A television talent show called *Star Search* came to Memphis.

Soul man

At his **audition** to join the television show the *Mickey Mouse Club*, Justin sang the classic soul hit, "When a Man Loves a Woman," by Percy Sledge (above).

At the *Mickey Mouse Club* , Justin (in the middle) joined other talented kids including Britney Spears (in the center of the front row).

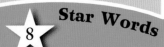
Star Words   tribute band musical group that plays another band's songs in a very similar style

Justin was chosen to appear on the show. He and his mother Lynn traveled to Orlando, Florida, to record the program. This was Justin's first television appearance. In the program he sang a country and western song, dressed in a cowboy hat. He did not win the competition, but he did get spotted by a **casting director**. The casting director was looking for children to appear on a television show called the *Mickey Mouse Club* (also known as *MMC*). Justin was invited to **audition** for the new series of the Disney program.

New Kids on the Block

New Kids on the Block (below) was the most famous boy band in the world in 1992. There was a lot of competition to be the "next big thing." Every audition saw kids lining up around the block for a chance. At the *MMC* auditions, Justin was one of just seven kids picked for the show out of 2,600 who tried out.

casting director person who picks out new talent to appear on television or in movies

Mickey Mouse Club

Justin joined Disney's *Mickey Mouse Club* in 1993. The show was in its sixth series. Some of the other "**Mouseketeers**" were already **veterans** of television. The main presenter, J.C. (Joshua Chasez), was only seventeen years old, but he was an experienced professional.

Melissa Joan Hart showed that being a Mouseketeer could lead the way to solo stardom.

The show

MMC was a remake of a show from the 1950s. It was different from other pop music programs because kids ran the show. It had stories, interviews, competitions, phone-ins, and pop news. It also featured the latest hits. The kid presenters did everything. They even performed **cover versions** of the latest hits live on the show. They had to look the part, dance the steps, and have great voices, too.

Teenage star

Melissa Joan Hart, better known as *Sabrina the Teenage Witch*, appeared in the early series of the *Mickey Mouse Club*.

A day's work

Being on the *MMC* might sound fun and glamorous, but it was also very hard work. The kids working with J.C. had to catch the school bus at 7 a.m. each morning. They then spent the morning in class with a special tutor at Disney's MGM studio. They spent the afternoon rehearsing and "doing wardrobe" to make them look just right for the occasion. This included clothes, hairstyle, and make-up—for the boys as well as the girls. Finally they performed the three-hour show in front of a live audience in the evening. This was a bit more than your average school day!

Star Words

veteran someone with a lot of experience in something

The *MMC* kids: That's Britney Spears sitting on the floor, Christina Aguilera on the right, and Justin at the back on the right.

Pop queens

Other young stars who appeared on the *MMC* included Britney Spears and Christina Aguilera (below). They are now two of the biggest female pop stars in the world. Christina once said: "We used to joke around backstage and say 'Whenever the show ends, we'll all go our separate ways and become stars.'"

cover version *recording of a song by a different performer*

Lives in Sync

Showbiz pressure

Justin was only fourteen years old when 'NSYNC was formed. Sometimes the pressures of show business were hard for him to handle. Justin says: "One day I broke down. I was crying and crying and I didn't know why."

Justin when he was fourteen.

The last series of the *Mickey Mouse Club* was in 1995, when Justin was fourteen. That left all of the **Mouseketeers** out of a job. Music had got Justin his part in the show. He was now a television star, but music was his first love. When the *MMC* came to an end, it was the perfect time for Justin to return to what he knew best.

J.C. and friends

While he was on the *MMC*, Justin became good friends with J.C. Chasez. J.C. had plans to form a boy band. Boy bands, like The Backstreet Boys, were very popular. Both Justin and J.C. had made contacts in the music business. They had the help of people, like the **choreographer** Wade J. Robson and the **producer** Pete Wylie. They started to try to make it in the music business.

Forming the band

Justin and J.C. moved back to Memphis from Florida, where the *MMC* had been filmed. They started looking for people to form a band with. They met up with Chris Kirkpatrick, who wanted to start a band with his friend, Joey Fatone. The four boys decided to try working together. Joey had a friend who was also interested in joining. The original fifth member was named Jason. He left after a short time. Justin then asked his old vocal coach, Bob Westbrook, if he knew anyone who might want to join.

Star Words

choreographer person who makes up dance routines for music videos and live performances

Bob put them in touch with Lance "Lansten" Bass. The boys decided on a name, 'NSYNC, and the band was complete!

The Backstreet Boys were huge in 1995, and 'NSYNC wanted the same sort of success.

Young stars

The New Kids on the Block had been huge in the early 1990s. By the mid-1990s, The Backstreet Boys were the fastest-selling boy band of all time. Pop music had had young stars before then, though. Two of Justin's biggest musical heroes are Michael Jackson and Stevie Wonder (above). They had both been child stars.

Hard work

Being a pop star might sound like fun, but it was hard work, too. 'NYSNC started out doing hundreds of **gigs** in schools, shopping malls, and tiny venues across Europe and Asia before returning to the United States to **promote** their first album. Recording in the studio could be long and boring. The video for "Tearin' Up My Heart" took 24 hours to film.

Five stars appeal

When Justin was not at school he was rehearsing in a warehouse with the other 'NSYNC boys. They recorded and sent out a video **demo**. To their delight, in 1996 they were taken on by Lou Pearlman and music manager Johnny Wright. Lou Pearlman was known in the music industry as "Big Poppa." These two men were behind the success of The Backstreet Boys.

Early days

From the summer of 1996 until the end of 1997, the band toured Europe, Africa, Asia, and Latin America. They also recorded their first album, 'NSYNC.

Star fact

Coming up with a name was one of the band's hardest decisions. It was Justin's mother, Lynn, who came up with the idea of taking the last letter of each of the members of the band: Justin, Chris, Joey, Jason (Lansten) and J.C.

Justin and the rest of the band often earned as many headlines for their dress sense as for their music!

It was not until the beginning of 1998 that they tried to get into the U.S. charts. They released the single, "I Want You Back," in March 1998. From that moment on their lives would never be the same.

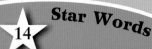

Star Words

14

a cappella music in which no instruments, just singing voices, are used

BAND BIOS

Joshua Chasez (J.C.)
Born: August 8, 1976, Washington, D.C.
Fun fact: J.C.'s first teenage crush was on Carrie Fisher. She played Princess Leia in the original *Star Wars* movies.

Christopher (Chris) Kirkpatrick
Born: October 17, 1971, Clarion, Pennsylvania
Fun fact: Chris was known for his piercings and bandannas. He also does *South Park* impressions.

Joseph (Joey) Fatone
Born: January 28, 1977, Brooklyn, New York
Fun fact: Joey was the eccentric in the band. He was famous for collecting *Superman* **memorabilia**.

James Lance (Lansten) Bass
Born: May 4, 1979, Clinton, Mississippi
Fun fact: Lance is fascinated by space travel. He wants to pay for a trip into outer space.

Many famous stars have recorded versions of the national anthem.

Singing stars

The band's first recording was an **a cappella** version of "The Star-Spangled Banner."

'NSYNC:
Chris,
J.C., Joey,
Lance, and
Justin.

memorabilia valuable objects from an event, movie, television show or famous person's life

'NSYNC on tour

Touring with 'NSYNC was very **intensive**. The band made 300 appearances in two tours over just one year. They had to have notes backstage to remind them what city they were in that night!

Hitting the big time

At the beginning of 1998, 'NSYNC were hardly known in the United States. The boys were selling millions of records across the rest of the world, though. All that changed with the release in the U.S. of their first single, "I Want You Back," in the spring. Then their first album, 'NSYNC, was released a few months later.

Summer sales

The boys spent the first months of the year **promoting** their music. It was in the summer that sales really took off. In one week in August, more than a quarter of a million copies of the album sold in just five days! They also went on tour with Janet Jackson.

Everywhere 'NSYNC went, thousands of fans were there to greet them.

No Strings Attached

The early success of 'NSYNC was overshadowed by what they achieved with the album *No Strings Attached* in 2000. It broke all the records. It sold more than a million copies on the first day it was released, and nearly 2.5 million in the first week! Tickets to the band's 52-date U.S. tour sold out on the first day that they went on sale. During the tour, the audience screamed so loudly that the boys had to wear earplugs!

Star Words   intensive busy; demanding, and challenging

'NYSNC spent long hours rehearsing to become a really exciting live band.

Devoted fans

The 1999 'NSYNC tour was very popular. Newspapers contained a story about fans who camped out in a dumpster for a week. They hoped that if they showed just what big fans they were, they might win tickets to the New York concert!

'NSYNC takes off

'NSYNC were having a great time. They sang at the Super Bowl. They appeared on *The Simpsons*. Their website was the most popular music site in the world. In 1999 they won Best New Group at the American Music Awards.

The boys were not only popular with fans. They also won awards from the music industry.

Going Solo

★ ★ ★ ★ ★ ★ ★ ★ ★ ★

Wonderful music

Stevie Wonder played the harmonica section of "Something Like You," from the *Celebrity* album. Justin had to ask him to play it again, as Stevie's harmonica was out of tune!

★ ★ ★ ★ ★ ★ ★ ★ ★ ★

'NYNSC's fourth album was called *Celebrity*. It was released in 2001 and sold nearly 2 million copies in the first week. This album was a turning point for Justin. He cowrote seven of the songs, and coproduced five. Even on the recording of the previous album, *No Strings Attached*, he had started to take notice of what the **producers** did to create the album's sound. This was something that he got very interested in.

Taking control

On *Celebrity*, Justin began to take even more control. He arranged for his hero Stevie Wonder to play harmonica on one of the songs. Justin also asked Pharrell Williams and Chad Hugo, of the respected hip hop producers, the Neptunes, to work on the album.

Album awards

The album received a **nomination** for a **Grammy** award for Best Pop Vocal Album. It was also nominated for the songs "Gone" (2002) and "Girlfriend" (2003).

Stevie Wonder lent his musical talents to *Celebrity*.

Star Words

nomination put forward as one of the people to win an award

Going solo gave Justin more freedom to make the music he wanted.

'NSYNC alone

Justin was not the only one in 'NSYNC who wanted to do his own thing. Joey hoped to make it as an actor on Broadway. Chris Kirkpatrick has signed on to manage the Dallas band, Ohno. J.C. has his own solo album, *Schizophrenic*.

★ ★ ★ ★ ★ ★ ★ ★ ★ ★

J.C. hopes to have his own solo success.

Leaving the band

There were rumors in newspapers and magazines that Justin was not happy in 'NSYNC and that the band was going to split. Justin never said that he wanted to leave, however. There was never an official break-up, but by 2002 he was writing a solo album.

Grammy award given at the most important annual music industry awards

7-Eleven

Justin wore a 7-Eleven cap in the video for "Like I Love You." The store sold tens of thousands of the caps in just a few weeks because of the video.

Justin in the recording studio with the Neptunes.

Whole new sound

Justin released the single "Like I Love You" in October 2002. It was **produced** by the Neptunes, who had worked on 'NSYNC's last album. The song was a musical mix. It had Mexican **acoustic** guitars. It had hip-hop. It even featured Clipse, a rap duo from Virginia. It also had an amazing video. In it Justin showed off his dance moves. This reminded many people of early **break dancing** moves. The single went to number eleven in the United States and number two in the United Kingdom.

"It's definitely a new sound—not just from me, but period. I think it's cool. I hope everybody else does."

Star Words

acoustic non-electronic instruments, a non-electric guitar, for example

Justin chooses the best people to work with, like Timbaland (left)—shown here with rappers Missy Elliot and Flavor Flav.

Michael Jackson

Michael Jackson is one of Justin's muscial heroes. His 1980s album, *Thriller*, still holds the world record for sales: more than 40 million. Justin says that Michael Jackson's music is an **inspiration** to him.

Michael Jackson's video for "Thriller" was the first of its kind.

First hits

Justin's first solo single was followed by two more hits. The first was "Cry Me a River." It was coproduced by the famous hip-hop producer, Timbaland. It was a number three hit in the United States and reached number two in the United Kingdom. The song was another mix of styles: R & B, hip-hop, slow rap, electronic horns, and strings. Justin's dance moves also made headlines, as well as his new **falsetto** singing style. The third single was cowritten with the Neptunes. It was called "Señorita" and was a mix of pop, funk, and **Latino**.

falsetto very high-pitched singing style
inspiration where you get your ideas from

All-star line-up

Justin's "sound" has changed a lot since his days with 'NSYNC. This is because of the people he has worked with. As we have already seen, when he made *Celebrity*, Justin worked with Stevie Wonder and the Neptunes. He had toured with another hero, Janet Jackson, as early as 1998.

Collaborators

In 2002, Justin **collaborated** with musicians from the world of R & B, hip-hop, dance, and pop. He even appeared in an Elton John video where he played Elton as a young man.

Childhood hero

Janet Jackson (above) was one of Justin's childhood heroes. She sings the backing vocals on Justin's track "(And She Said) Take Me Now."

Justin and Nelly proved that two can sometimes be better than one.

Star Words

collaborate work together with another singer or musician on a song

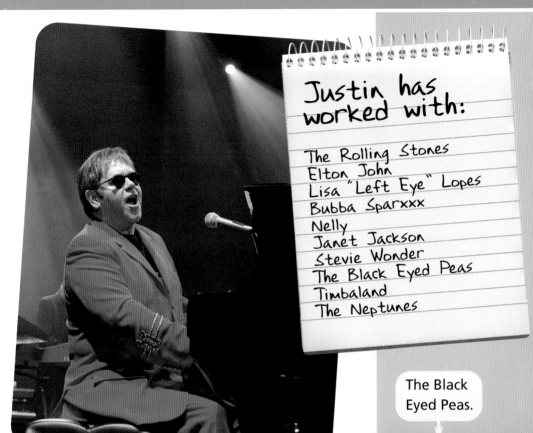

Justin has worked with:

The Rolling Stones
Elton John
Lisa "Left Eye" Lopes
Bubba Sparxxx
Nelly
Janet Jackson
Stevie Wonder
The Black Eyed Peas
Timbaland
The Neptunes

Justin has worked with world-famous musician Elton John.

The Black Eyed Peas.

Perhaps the most famous collaboration of all was with the rap star Nelly. Justin featured on the song "Work It," from Nelly's *Welcome to Nellyville* album.

Learning

Just before Justin's solo album, *Justified,* came out, he talked about his experience working with so many different artists. "It was so much fun, and I learned a lot about making music in a totally different way than I'm used to."

Justin has been in showbiz since he was eleven years old. He has had a lot of success. There have been awards, record album sales, and sell-out worldwide tours. There is the promise of many more in the future. So let's trace the highest points in Justin Timberlake's career—so far!

The highs

- First television show: Justin was a presenter on the *Mickey Mouse Club* from 1993 to 1995.
- Record sales: 'NSYNC sold millions of singles and albums. *No Strings Attached* sold 2.4 million copies in one week. That makes it the fastest selling album of all time!
- Going live: In 1999, 'NSYNC sold out five **consecutive** nights at New York's **prestigious** Radio City Music Hall.

Justin won three awards at the 2003 MTV Europe Awards.

★ ★ ★ ★ ★ ★ ★ ★ ★ ★

Awards

Justin's solo song, "Like I Love You," was nominated for Best Rap/Sung collaboration at the 2003 **Grammies**. Justin won the Best R & B category at the British MOBO awards in the same year.

★ ★ ★ ★ ★ ★ ★ ★ ★ ★

Justin had a lot of success when he was part of 'NYSNC.

Star Words   consecutive in a row or one after the other

They also sold out their 52-date U.S. tour the same year in just 8 hours!

• Large scale: In July 2003 Justin appeared at a live concert with the Rolling Stones. This was a charity event in Toronto, Canada. Justin performed in front of a crowd of 470,000!

• Giving something back: In May 2000, the Justin Timberlake Foundation awarded its first musical grant to Justin's old school.

• Awards: Since he has gone solo, Justin has appeared at almost every big awards ceremony. He has received many **nominations**. He is also the perfect awards host. In 2003, for example, he co-hosted the MTV Movie Awards.

Justin on Justin

"I've had good and bad moments as a pop star. My best moment was performing in the half-time show at the Super Bowl [in 2001], in front of 200,000 people. My worst moment is when I fell off the stage in Cologne, Germany. We had a new spotlight operator that night and both Joey Fatone and I fell off into the pit. It was really embarrassing."

Charity work

It is not only people in the music business who think highly of Justin. The Justin Timberlake Foundation helps to improve music education in schools. He was praised for this by former President Bill Clinton. He went to the White House and met the First Lady, Hillary Clinton.

Playing with the Rolling Stones saw Justin perform to one of his biggest audiences ever.

Style and Image

It is not just Justin's music that has changed since the early days with 'NSYNC. He has also changed his image. The young Justin was never happy with the way he looked. We have already mentioned that one of his childhood nicknames was "brillo pad." Justin says he once tried to cut all his hair off himself.

Standing out

As the lead singer of 'NSYNC, Justin was expected to stand out from the crowd. He was often made fun of for wearing baseball caps and flashy gold jewelry. When he tried something different, it was not always successful. His **cornrow** hairstyle is just one example!

Stylish?

Justin was not the only member of 'NSYNC with style problems. There was Joey with his **goatee** and Superman t-shirts. Then there was Chris with his piercings and tattoos.

The Justin of today might wish the bandanna had covered his whole head!

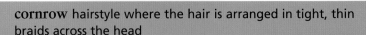

Star Words

cornrow hairstyle where the hair is arranged in tight, thin braids across the head

Justin's more mature look.

Eligible

In 1999, *People* magazine voted Justin the Most Beautiful Person of the Year. Britney Spears came second. Three years later, the same magazine named Justin America's Most **Eligible Bachelor** of the Year.

Justin looks great in a suit.

Growing up

Some people have also criticized Justin for copying Michael Jackson's look with a **fedora** hat and white gloves. His image has improved a lot, though. In his videos he has a more adult, urban, and hip-hop image. He has cropped his hair short. He is now often seen wearing fashionable suits from designer labels.

fedora old-fashioned type of hat made of soft felt, with a curled brim

Trickster

Many of Justin's fans might have spoken to him without knowing it. For a while his mobile phone number was almost the same as the number for a leading pizza chain. Justin often used to get orders for deliveries. Sometimes he played jokes on the callers, taking the orders before telling them they had the wrong number.

Justin has sold millions of records. He is often voted the most stylish or the sexiest man on the planet. These are not the only reasons why he is so popular, though. He also has a lot of charm and a good sense of humor. Many of his videos show this. The funny video for his **collaboration** with Nelly, "Work It," is one example. He has also appeared on British television with one of his favorite bands, The Flaming Lips, dressed in a furry animal costume!

The Flaming Lips are some of music's more unusual dressers.

Entertainer

Justin is a great entertainer. It is no wonder that **veteran** pop stars like The Rolling Stones asked him to play at their charity concert in Canada, or that Elton John wanted Justin to play him in a music video. Justin has even become the face and sound of an international fast-food chain.

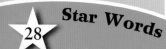

Star Words

spokesperson someone who represents a person or company

Keeping grounded

Justin knows how to keep his feet on the ground. Justin thanks his oldest and best childhood friend, Trace Ayala, for stopping him from being bigheaded. Justin says: "He makes me feel like I'm on Earth—he's unfazed by all this craziness."

For his live performances, Justin always gives his fans something different.

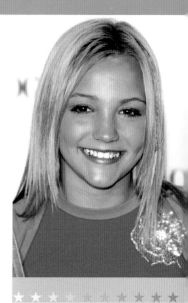

★ Star fact

In 2003 Justin was asked to perform for the Queen of England. A **spokesperson** for the royal family said: "It just goes to show that no woman on Earth is immune to his charms!"

Sister act

Justin has a sense of humor and never seems to lose his cool. In November 2002 he appeared on the Nickelodeon talk show *All That*. Britney Spears's little sister, Jamie Lynn (above), came on dressed as an 84-year-old bouncer. She catches Justin trying to sneak into a club. She pulls down his pants to reveal multi-colored underwear.

Personal Interests

Justin's first love is music. When he was in 'NSYNC, he called his band mates his "second family." Since he has gone solo, he has improved his piano and guitar skills. He has worked to improve his dance moves. He has also learned from his producer friends such as Timbaland and the Neptunes.

Remember your roots

Justin knows how lucky he has been. He has never forgotten where he comes from or the people who helped him be successful. In an interview with the *New York Post* in December 2000 he said: "I remember my parents always saying, 'Remember your roots. Whatever happens, remember your roots, remember where you came from.'"

Justin is a talented keyboard player, as well as a singer.

★ **Star Words**   fortunate lucky

Giving something back

Justin wants to help people who are less **fortunate** than he is. He set up the Justin Timberlake Foundation in 1999. This is a program that gives money for music and arts education in schools. In May 2000 the Foundation awarded its first grant to Justin's old elementary school.

New projects

Since he has changed his own image, Justin has been thinking about setting up his own line of clothing. He has also opened his own restaurant in Los Angeles. It is called Chi, and is inside the Hyatt Hotel on Sunset Boulevard.

Basketball

Justin is a good basketball player, and often plays in matches for charity.

Justin showed off his new dance moves at this concert in December 2003.

31

Justin loves his Harleys.

Work hard, play hard

Justin is a **dedicated** professional, but he still tries to find time to relax. He spends long days touring, recording, and receiving awards. He needs his time off, too.

Basketball magic

After music, Justin's biggest passion is probably basketball. He is a huge fan of the basketball legend, Michael Jordan, who retired in 2003. Justin's favorite basketball team is the Orlando Magic team.

Cars and bikes

Justin loves cars, and has a Mercedes M Class, a BMW roadster, a Dodge Viper, and a Cadillac Escalade. He also loves motorbikes. He gave Harley Davidsons to his mother and stepfather as presents. They were not the only bikes in the household. Justin says: "We have about seven now."

Justin is a big fan of Michael Jordan.

Star Words   dedicated hard-working

Throughout his childhood Justin collected basketball **memorabilia**. He is a good basketball player, too. His elementary school was impressed by his performances. After he left, they kept his number 12 shirt and did not let anyone else wear that number.

Justin at home

Justin now has his own house in the Hollywood Hills, but his Memphis home will always be the family home. There are **plasma screens** and video game consoles in almost every room. There is also a pinball machine.

On course

Justin can sometimes be spotted playing golf, one of his new-found interests. His $8 million house in the Hollywood Hills is designed in a Mexican style. It stands on 10 acres of land, and has a tennis court.

Justin on TV

Although music is his first job, Justin is also interested in acting. He made a guest appearance on *Sabrina the Teenage Witch* in 1996. He also appeared in the television movie *Model Behavior* in 2000. There are a lot of rumors that Justin will appear in movies. He has not denied them all!

Golf is a relaxing escape from Justin's hectic life.

plasma screen modern flat screen often used for laptop computer screens and large-screen televisions

Media Spotlight

Beyoncé is another solo success. She won five **Grammy** awards in 2004.

Solo success

Justin is not the first singer to become even more famous after going solo. Beyoncé Knowles was already a huge star with Destiny's Child. Since she released her own solo album, she has become even more successful.

Justin has never been camera shy. He often admits that he feels most comfortable when he has an audience. Before he appeared in the *Mickey Mouse Club* on television, he had tried out at every music **audition** he could get to. You may remember that he sang in a boy band at his elementary school. Justin loves the camera, and the camera also loves him.

Fan favorite

When Justin joined 'NSYNC he was the youngest member of the band. He was only fourteen years old. Some of his band mates were much older

Star fact

When he was with 'NSYNC, Justin and his band mates made a **cameo** appearance on the cartoon show, *The Simpsons*.

and more experienced. By 1999, Justin had become the favorite with the fans, as well as the press. Justin never meant to attract more attention than the other boys, but in every 'NSYNC interview, half of the questions were for him alone.

Famous girlfriend

From 2000 to 2002, Justin and his equally famous girlfriend were one of pop's most glamorous couples. His relationship with Britney Spears made Justin even more popular with the **media**. During those years, though, it was Britney who was the center of attention. She was much more famous than Justin.

Star Words

cameo short appearance in a television program, video, or movie

In the spotlight

Now Justin has become the "most **eligible bachelor** in the world." He has a best-selling album and singles. He has award-winning videos. He has had movie offers. His face is on magazine covers. He has a new style of music and a new fashion look. He is now much more famous than the other 'NSYNC members. He gets the sort of **publicity** that Britney does.

Justin is always an impressive live performer.

Joker

Justin once appeared on the MTV hidden camera show, *Punk'd*. He played a joke on rock singer Kelly Osbourne (below). He arranged for record executives to have a meeting with the rock star. They told Kelly that she had to change her image to look more like Christina Aguilera or Britney Spears!

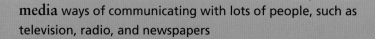

media ways of communicating with lots of people, such as television, radio, and newspapers

Engaged?

In July 2000 a British newspaper claimed that Justin had proposed to Britney. Apparently he put a $48,000 engagement ring on her finger while they were sipping coffee in a cafe. This, however, was never confirmed!

Celebrity teamwork

Britney Spears is a name often **associated** with Justin. They met when they were both new **Mouseketeers** on the *Mickey Mouse Club*. They became friends. They played ping pong in between shooting for the program.

Early friendship

After the *MMC* series ended in 1995, Britney went to New York. Justin returned to Memphis and went back to school.

★ Star fact

While 'NSYNC was becoming the biggest boy band in the world, Britney made it huge. Her single, "Baby One More Time," was a big hit in 1998. Her album of the same name sold more than 20 million copies.

Britney and the 'NYSNC boys toured together in the early days.

Star Words   associated to do with or mentioned along with

Justin and Britney finally admitted that they were an item.

It was only after he had joined the band 'NSYNC that he began to see Britney again. She had started her own music career. She even supported the boys on tour.

Going public

Justin and Britney were old friends. They often went to **premieres** and music awards together. Soon the rumors started that they were an item. At first the couple denied they were more than just friends. Then Britney cracked under the pressure. In an interview with the music magazine *Rolling Stone* in May 2000, she admitted that she and Justin had kissed. When she realized what she had done she laughed and said: "Oh my gosh, my manager is going to kill me." Finally they had "gone public."

Young love

Justin and Britney seemed like the perfect couple. Their families were happy about the relationship. Although it took them years actually to go out, it looked as if it had been love at first sight. When Justin was just twelve, he told his grandmother, Sadie, that he thought he would marry Britney one day.

premiere first showing of a movie, often with celebrities invited

Celebrity couples

Some famous couples do stay together, but many cannot survive the **media** attention. Look at all the problems that Jennifer Lopez and Ben Affleck had when they were engaged. Couples often say that it is hard to stay together when their jobs mean that they are apart for most of the time.

Double trouble

Justin and Britney seemed to be the "dream" couple of the pop world. Wherever they went together, pictures of them appeared in newspapers and magazines. There were problems for them, though. Britney and Justin were often on tour in distant parts of the world. They worked long hours. This meant they could not spend much time together.

Splitting up

It started to appear that Justin and Britney were not happy. At the **premiere** of her movie, *Crossroads*, in March 2002, Britney said that she was "not in an **intense** relationship with anyone." There were even rumors that she had started going out with someone else. No one apart from Britney and Justin really knows what happened, but it became clear that they were no longer a couple.

Jennifer Lopez and Ben Affleck had lots of problems with the media.

⭐ Star fact

Justin had a "pet name" for Britney—"Pinky." He calls her "Pinky" on the **liner notes** to the 'NSYNC album *Celebrity*. This is because of the ring she wears on her little finger, or "pinky." Britney called Justin "stinky!" No explanation needed!

Star Words

liner notes notes inside a CD booklet. Performers use them to thank all the people who have helped them.

What went wrong?

Justin refused to say exactly what went wrong between him and Britney. In an interview with the British magazine *Marie Claire* in May 2003 he said: "No one knows what went on between Britney and me except us. . .we're friends now. We're not mad at each other."

The cameras followed Justin and Britney everywhere.

Alyssa Milano was one of the women seen out with Justin after Britney.

Single again

Justin might have gone solo in 2002, but that does not mean he was alone. There seemed to be a lot of girls who wanted to go out with him. He was seen out with the actress Alyssa Milano. He was also seen with Janet Jackson and 'NSYNC dancer Jenna Dewan.

Big seller

Justified sold more than 3 million copies by the end of 2003. It also earned Justin respect from within the music industry. His mom said in an interview with *Rolling Stone* magazine in December 2003: "At the VMAs, when he won the award [for Best Male Video] and Eminem and 50 Cent stood up to applaud, that left such an impression on him."

By the spring of 2002, Justin was single again. It also looked as if he might be going solo as a musician. He and the other 'NSYNC boys went to the Cannes Film Festival that year. They talked about their plans for a joint movie project. By that time, Justin was already preparing to record a solo album. Then he had an accident while rehearsing for a show in Toronto. He broke a bone in his foot. The accident gave Justin a chance to take some time off. He returned to his family home in Memphis to get better and have some time to himself.

Even in that tracksuit, there is no way Justin is going to escape the press!

Taking a break

The accident delayed Justin's solo projects, but it also gave him time to rest and decide what he wanted to do with his life. What he wanted to do was to work on his new material and new sound.

First singles

By the end of the summer Justin was very much back in the **media**. His first two singles, "Like I Love You" and "Cry Me a River" were hits across the globe. His album, *Justified,* made him one of the hottest solo artists in the world.

Justin out with his mom.

Justin's mom

Justin and his mom often go out together. Justin has admitted that she often comes home later at night than he does! In an interview with the *Herald* newspaper, Justin explained: "We have a very special relationship. She's always been there beside me."

Justin and Chris Kirkpatrick show the press that the 'NSYNC "family" have never quarreled.

Now and Then

Music

What will Justin's music be like in the future? Justin's friend and producer, Timbaland, made a **prediction** as early as 2002: "He's about to become so much more famous than he already is that it's going to blow people away. The stuff he's doing is so cool and revolutionary."

Justin has been on front covers of fashion, style, and music magazines from all around the world. He has been the lead singer in the fastest-selling band of all time. He was one half of one of the biggest celebrity couples on the planet. Now he is a huge solo star. He has written for, and **collaborated** with, the biggest stars in the music business. So what now for Justin?

Hot property

A couple of months after the release of *Justified*, Justin said: "I think this album has established my identity. I think this was my coming out party." Justin is certainly hot property now. Many of the world's top artists have asked to work with him. He has worked with the chart-topping hip-hop group The Black Eyed Peas. He has won some of the top music awards in the world.

Not just music

Justin is not only making music. He has signed a contract as a television **sports correspondent** to talk about basketball, his favorite sport. He has also opened his own restaurant. That is a busy schedule!

Justin in the video for "I'm Lovin' It."

On screen

Justin may be appearing on screen. He was sent a script to play the role of Jimmy Olsen in the next *Superman* movie.

Star Words

prediction what someone thinks might happen in the future

He has said he would like to be in a movie version of the musical *Rent*. Whatever Justin does next, one thing is clear—he is set to become an even bigger star than he is now.

Being solo does not mean you cannot be a team player, as Justin showed with The Black Eyed Peas.

Justin and Cameron Diaz trying to avoid the attention of the cameras.

Love

After the split with Britney, Justin claimed that he needed a break. That has not stopped the rumors. He has been linked with models, actresses, and singers. The only person he has admitted to going out with is the movie star, Cameron Diaz.

sports correspondent someone who comments on sports on television, radio, or in newspapers

Find Out More

Books

Johns, Michael-Anne. *Pop People: Justin*. New York: Scholastic, 2000

Netter, Matt. *NSYNC with Justin*. New York: Simon Pulse, 1999

Roach, Martin. *Justin Timberlake: The Unofficial Book*. New York:Virgin Books, 2003

DVD/VHS

Live from London (2003)

Justified (2003)

Startrax: Justin Timberlake/'NSYNC (2003)

'NSYNC – Popodyssey (2001)

'NSYNC: Making the Tour (2000)

'NSYNC: Live From Madison Square Gardens (2000)

Discography

Albums

Justified (2002)

Singles

"Work It" (Nelly and Justin Timberlake) (2003)

"Rock Your Body" (2003)

"Señorita" (2003)

"Cry Me a River" (2002)

"Like I Love You" (2002)

Albums with 'NSYNC

Celebrity (2001)

No Strings Attached (2000)
The Winter Album (1998)
'NSYNC (1998)

Website search tips

There are billions of pages on the Internet so it can be difficult to find exactly what you are looking for. If you just type in "movie" on a search engine, like Google, you will get a list of millions of web pages. These search skills will help you find useful websites more quickly:

• know exactly what you want to find out
• use simple keywords, not whole sentences
• use two to six keywords in a search
• be precise, only use names of people, places, or things
• if you want to find words that go together, put quote marks around them
• use the "+" sign to add certain words, for example, typing "Justin Timberlake + albums" into the search box will find web pages about Justin's albums.

Glossary

a cappella music in which no instruments, just singing voices, are used

acoustic non-electronic instruments, a non-electric guitar, for example

associated to do with or mentioned along with

audition interview for a musician or actor, where they show their skills

bluegrass music that combines Irish and Scottish traditional music with that of the African-American slaves

break dancing energetic form of street dancing popular in the 1980s. Break dancers would often compete against each other to see whose moves were the best.

cameo short appearance in a television program, video or movie

casting director person who picks out new talent to appear on television or in movies

choreographer person who makes up dance routines for music videos and live performances

collaborate work together with another singer or musician on a song

consecutive in a row or one after the other

cornrow hairstyle where the hair is arranged in tight, thin braids across the head

cover version recording of a song by a different performer

dedicated hard-working

demo examples of songs recorded by musicians who are just starting out. They often send demos to record producers to try and get noticed.

eligible bachelor single man who is popular with women

falsetto very high-pitched singing style

fedora old-fashioned type of hat made of soft felt, with a curled brim

fortunate lucky

gig live performance

goatee beard that covers the chin and moustache area, leaving the neck and cheeks bare

Grammy award given at the most important annual music industry awards

icon important or famous person that you look up to and try to be like

inspiration where you get your ideas from

intense very emotional

intensive busy, demanding and challenging

Latino from Latin America. Popular music styles include salsa, mambo, and son Cubano

liner notes notes inside a CD booklet. Performers use them to thank all the people who have helped them.

media ways of communicating with lots of people, such as television, radio, and newspapers

memorabilia valuable objects from an event, movie, television show or famous person's life

Mouseketeers name given to the young stars of the *Mickey Mouse Club*

nomination put forward as one of the people to win an award

plasma screen modern flat screen often used for laptop computer screens and large-screen televisions

prediction what someone thinks might happen in the future

premiere first showing of a movie, often with celebrities invited

prestigious of great value; highly regarded or thought of

producer person in charge of making a record, film or television show

production arranging and mixing the music when recording a song

promote tell people about a new product

spokesperson someone who represents a company

sports correspondent someone who comments on sports on television, radio, or in newspapers

suburb outskirts of a city where people live

trademark something that is typical about a person

tribute band musical group that plays another band's songs in a very similar style

veteran someone with a lot of experience in something

Index